# Two Trees

## by PETER MCDONNELL

Mc Graw Hill **Macmillan**
**McGraw-Hill**

This is a desert ironwood tree.

These are coast redwood trees.

Desert ironwood tree with flowers

This tree grows where it is dry.
Its **roots** get water from under
the ground.

Coast redwood tree

This tree grows where it rains.
Its roots get water from the
wet **soil**.

Both trees need sunlight to make food.

Food and water make trees grow tall.

# Glossary

 **roots** (ROOTS) plant parts that take in water *(page 4)*

 **soil** (SOYL) the top part of the ground in which plants grow *(page 5)*

# Index